THREE MAGPIES PERCHED IN A TREE

Glenn Shea

CURRENCY PRESS
The performing arts publisher

CURRENT THEATRE SERIES

First published in 2024
by Currency Press Pty Ltd,
Gadigal Land, Suite 310, 46–56 Kippax Street, Surry Hills, NSW 2010, Australia
enquiries@currency.com.au
www.currency.com.au

in association with La Mama

Copyright: *Three Magpies Perched in a Tree* © Glenn Shea, 2024.

COPYING FOR EDUCATIONAL PURPOSES

The Australian *Copyright Act 1968* [Act] allows a maximum of one chapter or 10% of this book, whichever is the greater, to be copied by any educational institution for its educational purposes provided that that educational institution [or the body that administers it] has given a remuneration notice to Copyright Agency [CA] under the Act.

For details of the CA licence for educational institutions contact CA, 12 / 66 Goulburn Street, Sydney, NSW, 2000; tel: within Australia 1800 066 844 toll free; outside Australia 61 2 9394 7600; fax: 61 2 9394 7601; email: memberservices@copyright.com.au

COPYING FOR OTHER PURPOSES

Except as permitted under the Act, for example a fair dealing for the purposes of study, research, criticism or review, no part of this book may be reproduced, stored in a retrieval system, or transmitted in any form or by any means without prior written permission. All enquiries should be made to the publisher at the address above.

Any performance or public reading of *Three Magpies Perched in a Tree* is forbidden unless a licence has been received from the author or the author's agent. The purchase of this book in no way gives the purchaser the right to perform the play in public, whether by means of a staged production or a reading. All applications for public performance should be addressed to the author c / - Currency Press.

Typeset by Brighton Gray for Currency Press.
Cover image by Darren Gill; photo shows Glenn Shea.

Currency Press acknowledges the Traditional Owners of the Country on which we live and work. We pay our respects to all Aboriginal and Torres Strait Islander Elders, past and present.

A catalogue record for this book is available from the National Library of Australia

Contents

Foreword: Where Do Plays Come From?   v

THREE MAGPIES PERCHED IN A TREE   1

Theatre Program at the end of the playtext

Foreword: Where Do Plays Come From?

In 2009, I directed a production of Harold Pinter's *The Birthday Party* for Melbourne Theatre Company with a largely Indigenous cast (all but one of the roles). There is a marked affinity between the regional idioms Pinter originally intended for this play, and the Australian vernacular as spoken by First Nations actors. The critical reception of the show was, to put it mildly, depressing. The arts media have come a long way since that frankly racist response, though perhaps not as far as they like to think. I had worked with Glenn Shea on the premiere of *Who's Afraid of the Working Class?* in 1997, when he was the first Aboriginal actor to graduate from NIDA. In *The Birthday Party,* he took the part of McCann and turned in, as he always does, a tour de force of character acting, that unmistakable combination of bulk, strength and oh so delicate physicality, a dancer in the body of a professional athlete. One of the things Glenn said to me after we got to know each other better was 'I don't fight. I *don't* fight'.

My heart leapt when I heard the words. It flagged a search for empathy and understanding, tributary streams flowing into the broader river of healing and reconciliation. In the quarter of a century that Glenn and I have been friends, I have had glimpses of that river, moments both big (Kevin Rudd's apology to the Stolen Generation in 2008) and small (the first reading of *Three Magpies Perched in a Tree* on Sorry Day in 2012) when some national and historical transformation seemed within reach. Yet somehow the moments dissipated, and the river slipped from view. This is how it felt after we opened *The Birthday Party* to wild audience applause that just went on and on, and then read those stupid, stupid reviews.

Halfway through the run, Glenn told me he had written a play, and asked me if I would look at it. He was working as a youth justice worker, in a world not only did I know nothing about, but which I could barely conceive. It read like a filmscript, with scene following scene in linear fashion, and visual settings carefully described. It was gripping. But it was not a stage play, and I said so. I had some dramaturgical notes I generated when co-developing *Angela's Kitchen* with Paul Capsis the year before. Drawing on my time as Literary Adviser at MTC, they were basically a list of choices a playwright could make when creatively shaping their play. I gave them to Glenn and thought it would be months—if ever—that I saw his script again. Yet by the end of *The Birthday Party's* season three weeks later, he handed me a complete revision astonishing in its scope and sophistication. There was no doubt about it. He had a play.

Two things then happened which helped me grasp the world Glenn lived and breathed but that was so alien to me. First, I went to hear him talk at Parkville Youth Detention Centre. Located around the corner from where I live in Brunswick, I had passed this facility many times without thinking much about it. In his self-deprecating way, Glenn invited me to a briefing he was giving to a mixture of detention staff and outreach workers. What I remember of that meeting was its casually professional atmosphere and how Glenn, who I knew as an actor, was a figure of authority and service. How natural that change— which was no change, because he was always thus—seemed. My mind wobbled slightly on its bearings. Beyond the outer room in which we sat, its drab paintwork and worn-out furniture, suffering and confusion bloomed. I couldn't see or hear it. But I sensed it now.

A few weeks later, Glenn asked me to accompany him as he did the rounds of his clients in Geelong. It was a brilliant, clear autumn morning, the sky a perfect duck-egg blue. As we drove down from Melbourne, Glenn chatted about who we would see, what their problems were, and the main purpose of his job: to keep these young men and women *out* of the justice system; to intervene in such a way that the tragic trifecta of court, sentencing and incarceration did not wreck their vulnerable, evolving lives. Some jobs exist to achieve goals external to themselves. Youth justice work exists to make the job itself redundant.

Like the Parkville Detention Centre meeting, the day was, on the surface, muted, ordinary. The struggles in which these individuals were embroiled were not readily apparent. I grew up in London where deprivation is on immediate display. The inner-city suburbs of the Thatcher era—Brixton, Notting Hill, Seven Sisters, Peckham—were visibly ravaged, badlands of waste and despair. Poverty in Australia is more in the background, and especially concentrated in the regions.

You have to know where to look for it, then hold steady when you see it. The temptation is to turn away, to retreat to the 'relaxed and comfortable' Australia that Prime Minister John Howard urged us to live in, but many of us just don't.

In the months following, the play, now officially titled *Three Magpies Perched in a Tree,* was officially 'developed'. What does this involve? In essence, doing whatever pushes the writing forward to the next draft. Every few weeks I would drive to Geelong, along that flat, featureless highway, to an airy, well-lit room where, with a small group of actors, a composer, and a choreographer, the latest version of the script would be read and discussed. In between times, I would wield the pen—the dramaturg's weapon of choice—the aim being to better-ize Glenn's dialogue without compromising his intentions, choice of form or authorial voice.

We are friends still, so I must have been okay at this. However, the play was already in good nick after that first remarkable revision, so the main task was to understand what he had brought into being. This is a more egalitarian exercise than one might think. Plays are public objects. They have a literary dimension, like poems and novels, but they engage on a collective level, first with the theatre artists who perform them, next with the audiences who see them. So we talked in collaborative fashion, with Glenn, as surprised as any of us that such a beautiful play now existed, about the truths he was wanted to communicate.

Think of plays as nets, spinning gossamer threads of stories, characters, and words that attempt to capture, spectrally, the hearts and minds of living artists. It is a paradox every theatre person knows: we are most ourselves when trying to be someone else, the world beyond who we are showing us more clearly who we really are.

Think of *Three Magpies* as one such net, its non-linear jumps and story fragments given propulsive power by the need to touch on things easy to miss and hard to witness. It is 'poetic', if we mean by this over-used and trite term, that its dialogue has powerful resonance, like a stone thrown into a deep well, the echo of its splash lasting long after its initial impact. There are stories within stories in *Three Magpies*, and song. There is a narrator figure, Peter ('the rock'), holding its different parts together, who is, I suppose, Glenn, but also the Stage Manager in *Our Town,* the Common Man in *Man for All Seasons,* and Homer in *The Iliad*. In other words, while *Three Magpies* is original in what it says and shows, and in its construction, it taps a long tradition of theatre craft wherein reported and presented action meld together in seamless fashion. This allows the playwright great freedom to move through time and space to plumb the mystery of human experience, and express his shard of it, that for Glenn is so sharp and fierce, but for which he has the heart to bear witness.

And behind Homer, for tens of thousands of years, a longer tradition still. There is in *Three Magpies* several Dreamtime stories, recounted between the contemporary ones, hope among the ruins. There is an absence of didacticism about their telling, as indeed there is about the play overall. Despite its elliptical form, winding its story fragments back onto themselves, like a giant ball of wool, its goal is to be as direct as possible about things about which it is impossible to be direct. The Dreamtime stories are a net-thread trying to capture what is glimpsed at the eye's edge, the part standing proxy for the whole, the world of the play standing proxy for the world. In the original program note for the 2012 NAIDOC Week reading, I wrote:

> Drama is a tool fashioned to do a job. With *Three Magpies* that job is devastatingly simple: to tell the truth. It's simple because it's a one-stop aim. No extraneous agenda needs be considered, no desire to weight one side of the story. Peter is a man divided in himself, his loyalties and his belief in what he's doing. No attempt is made to hide this, to present him as a paper hero. Perhaps that's why there are three of him on stage. It's devastating because to convey the reality of young Aboriginal people today means invoking a tsunami of social and historical factors that defy easy explanation. Cause and effect spin out in long dysfunctional chains that extend over centuries. Peter tries to show the reasons why the terrible things around him are happening. But he knows too much, and this knowledge exacts a terrible personal price. However, there's another kind of narrative in the play: the Dreamtime stories. These exist in positive counterpoint to the tales of contemporary destruction. Modern drama doesn't require much exposition. The Dreamtime stories aren't worked into the play in an arty way. They are there

because they need to be, because Peter and us, the audience, spiritually require them. They are a reminder of what's been lost, but not just that. They exist as sacred things to get the suffering soul through the benighted day.

Another tired, over-used word: *hope*. Since the Covid pandemic, Australia has managed to spruik hope as an ideal without doing much to realise it in practical terms. *Three Magpies* was written in a challenging time. We live in a paralysed one. We know the problems we face. Yet we do little to address them. The major industry in Australia right now feels like the making of excuses. As the past comes back to haunt the nation, the disattention once applied to Glenn's young offenders is today a general strategy.

'I don't fight.' Anger, in its context and in proportion, is to be respected. But anger by itself is not enough. The great question is 'Where to next?' and here hope is essential. If we cannot imagine change, individually and collectively, then we will not change. The impulse must proceed the act, else the act will be unrealised. Again, here, drama shows its worth. It helps us rethink our lives even as we are trying to live them.

Towards the end of *Three Magpies* there is a story-fragment—one of the shortest—when Peter is in the pub, perhaps after a long day, perhaps after the closure of the youth justice intervention program itself. A young boy comes up to him, and

> I am sitting in a pub when I hear a voice say …
> [*As Young Voice*] Hello Peter
> He was a young man.
> I don't recognise him, but I play along, and he introduces me to his mother and his girlfriend.
> [*As Mother*] Hello
> [*As Girlfriend*] Hello
> And he says
> [*As Young Voice*] Do you recognise me?
> I look at him but still can't place him.
> [*As Young Voice*] I am from the place where you have just been.
> And I stare at him, and his mother says …
> [*As Mother*] I want to thank you for changing my son's life.

And the boy had become a man
and he shakes my hand.
[*As Young Voice*] You changed my life.
You're welcome.

Silence.

    As a dramaturg, I have developed many plays. Some I have been fortunate enough to direct as well. Theatre is a rough and tumble business. Some dramas work, others don't. Some dreadful work is programmed, and some good, and more to the point interesting, plays are left on the shelf. But in my four decades of working in Australian theatre I have never seen the sort of worm-hearted slight and avoidance that I saw extended to the two plays of Glenn's I was involved with, *Three Magpies Perched in a Tree* and *MI:WI 3027*. Both should have been staged, if not my me, then by *someone* and if not by someone, then most certainly by me. They have received La Mama productions, the first in 2023, the second in 2024. But this is long after the net was first cast, and the shame and frustration of that burns me like cold fire.

    Glenn is more even-tempered, even cheerful, about the situation, as he always is. The past is dead and gone. It is the future that matters. The publication of these plays communicates another truth theatre people know: the show is not over until it's over. While Glenn continues to write, his unique voice continues to thrive and grow. *My* sincerest hope is that one day I can give that voice directorial life.

Julian Meyrick

Three Magpies Perched in a Tree was first presented to the Wathaurong Aboriginal Community in 2012 at the Courthouse Theatre in Djillong (Geelong). The first production was produced as part of *An Indigenous Trilogy* by La Mama and THE STORYTELLER® at La Mama Courthouse Theatre, Carlton, Melbourne (Naarm), on the traditional custodial lands of the Woi-Wurrung and Boon-Wurrung Language Groups, on 8 November 2022 with the following cast:

PERFORMER	Glenn Shea
CREATION STORY VOICEOVERS	Uncle Jack Charles

Producers, LA MAMA Tessa Spooner and THE STORYTELLER® Elder Glenn Shea
Director, Elder Glenn Shea
Dramaturg, Julian Meyrick
Associate director, Kirsty M Reilly
Stage manager, Kelly Harris
Assistant stage manager, Lauren Thuys
Designer, Valentina Serebrennikova
Lighting designer, Bronwyn Pringle
Sound designer, DE
Projectionist, Simon Bowland
Animation / 2D, Mia-Bijou Gollan Reilly-Shea

CHARACTER

PETER

NOTES

When Peter is talking to the system, he is talking to the camera in the room.

Peter does not know his father.

The four creation stories can be either voiceover or an actor. In this version they are voiceovers.

Peter's sanctuary has a seat.

PHILOSOPHY—Glenn's Theory

BLAK THEATRE	WESTERN THEATRE
Country.	Stage.
Language.	Script.
Lore.	Protocols.
Kinship.	Ensemble.
Ceremony.	Performance.

Directors: in your direction, please use your imagination. You have my permission.

—*G.S.*

COMMUNITY NOTICE: Aboriginal and Torres Strait Islander viewers are warned that the following book contains images and names of deceased ATSI persons.

This play text went to press before the end of rehearsals and may differ from the play as performed.

PROLOGUE

Incarceration of the spirit. Shadows talking. Thousands of voices. Sense of time ticking (clock). Hourglass drips salt throughout the show. Low energy, static rumbling, distorted ocean, wind. Campfire.

Enter PETER.

PETER: Father.

    I came here from another place.

    Though I know it like the back of my hand, I have lived and seen the world, travelling a lonely road.

    Father, I have been many things though at times I did not know who I was. I have lived in the depths of hell fighting demons, too many to count. So, I wake up in the morning and accept the challenge of a brand-new day, not knowing what it will bring.

    I love this place. I love the water and the breeze as it whips in from the ocean. I love the sunrise and the colours that light up the morning sky. I love hearing the crashing of the waves as they hit the shore and the wind as it dances through one of the oldest instruments in the world.

    I have heard the sounds and the rhythms of the young, the bursts of tune that grab their attention. I have heard the beat as it beats, and it beats and it beats preying on the minds of the innocent. Hollow sounds, shallow words turning the world to chaos.

    I have heard the cries of the young and seen their faces. I have sat with them as they lie with tubes in their arms from the damage they have done.

    I have picked them up from streets of loneliness, wandering in the darkness with a shimy by their side. I have seen their faces and smelt their bodies from the clothes they wear and never change.

    Father, I have seen and felt their anger and have seen and felt them ever so slightly smile a real smile. I have seen their thoughts change to the possibility of a life beyond their bars. I have seen them stand up and say what they think. I have seen them dance because it's part of who they are and embrace an opportunity. But rarely have I seen them embrace a touch of love from their family.

I have seen the system fail them because the statistics say they are not the ones we are going to help today.

I have seen the system make excuses.

I have seen the system feel good about itself, for it can tick a box.

So, when it comes to the heart it is just a ticking clock.

I love this place. I love the water and the breeze as it whips in from the ocean. I love the sunrise and the colours which light up the morning sky. I love hearing the crashing of the waves as they hit the shore.

I love my sanctuary, my escape from the world.

Pause.

I love my silence.

WELCOME TO MY WORLD

Dark place. Continuous soft beat. PETER *draws a circle with white salt.*

PETER: I'm hungry, can I have a piece of that pie? I want to eat.

> *We see the shape of a pie.*

Well? Can I have this piece?
SYSTEM: No.

> PETER *cuts it up into pieces of a pie.*

PETER: Can I have this slice? I'm hungry.
SYSTEM: Stop talking.
PETER: Hey, I hope you enjoy that!

> PETER *wipes away the pie.*
>
> *Silence.*

If you thought the face of the world was beautiful think again. Lost, desolate, desperate: we live in a society with no understanding of the issues that impact on our lives, that tear at the fabric of our souls.

That plague our minds like tricks and thievery. When a child walks out the door they meet the devils that dance within. The chance play of winds, winds that decide who loses and who wins.

Wake up. Wake up and smell the fear bestowed upon us, while others revel in the world of illusion, their escape negated by what they will not see.

Wake up. We have passed the year in which to safely live. Tick tock, tick tock your child is about to drop, falling uncontrollably into a sea of worms, slithering silently into despair.

I know it. I've seen it. I've lived it. God bless this hell though it rips the heart out of those who innocently look on.

What are you going to do? Believe in only good and never evil as the world rotates on a cusp?

How shallow is the thinking which drives the victim's victim to despair.

Welcome to the jungle.

May you beat the drum of loneliness.

All I'm going to share is the stories I have lived. You can analyse them, dream them, replay them. But you will never know the dark side of our reality until you understand them. I'm gone, for I was never here. Welcome to my world. Let's kneel in prayer.

I. CREATION ANCESTOR STORY

Shadow movement.

VOICEOVER: A long time ago in the time of Creation, our Creation ancestors formed the land and gave it life, and rituals to keep it living. They also gave us the law and rules to live by. Creation explains the origins of the universe, how nature works, and people too. Now with people, there was kinship and family life, and the law between men and women. We are responsible for the people, the land, and the spirits.

All Creation ancestors had power and could change into any form they wanted. After working on the Creation some went back into the land and others went into the sky. The sun and moon and all the stars are the Creation figures. All through the land there are Creation tracks.

You can see the Creation ancestor at their most powerful in sacred sites. When you go to these places, and feel yourself a part of them, you know why the animals, birds, fish, and plants are so powerful. Performing the rituals and the stories, both sacred and public, keeps these places alive.

A person's Creation is their identity, their belonging, and their place in the world. It is where their spirit comes from, and where it must return. Creation is forever, life and death, without beginning or end. It is beyond words. It is the song of the universe, the rhythm of the land.

Creation is the life of the spirit, the imagination. It is told with art, poetry, music, storytelling, drama, and dance. Most of all, the Creation ties and binds people to the land that owns them.

JESSIE AND RACHEL'S STORY

Enter PETER.

PETER: I am driving down the road. It's a quiet afternoon and the world appears surreal in the rear-view mirror.

'Thanks for coming. We have a situation. Our case workers have completed the research process on members of a family. We have to remove a child.'

I see the baby seat.

We were wondering if you could do it for us. Makes it easier on them, you know, friendlier. Otherwise, we have to do it the hard way. Do you have the baby seat?

I see the baby seat to the left of me in the back.

I am now part of what was and what is going to be.

I stare at the baby seat, and I see myself.

The car is stopped. The car is stopped.

I arrive at the house and walk up the driveway. I know why I am here. I have sat in meetings discussing the implosion of families and the need to do something for the future of our children. Then the wheel turns and I am here knocking at a door.

I have been to this house many times. Julie and her daughter Jessie live here. Jessie's cousin Rachel stays over. They don't play with dolls or skipping ropes. They smoke pot, pop pills and drink with their relations. They are twelve and thirteen years old.

[*As Subconscious, an echo*] Peter.

Most times when people come out of lock-up, they are clean. No drugs, no alcohol, they are in a routine. They come out of jail, and some want a second chance. But if you have a big family and most of them are involved in crime, it's hard to ignore the constant voices.

Come on, come on, come on, distract and divert, come on.

At first, they are still in lock-up routine, wake at sunrise, shite, shower, shave.

Shite, shower, shave, shite, shower, shave

But when they look in the mirror, they say 'What's next?'

What's next?

Now there is no routine. Time passes from day to night, night to day. They're up at sunrise, but this time when they look in the mirror, they hear the sound of a twist top coming off a bottle and the constant voices are louder.

Distract and divert, distract, and divert.

Come on!

Shopping centres, bottle shops, churches, day and night, night or day, doesn't matter and if you're elderly or weak someone's watching and when the moment is right, they'll knock on the door and ask to use the toilet.

Distract and divert.

And threaten for a key card and a pin number, then go to the bank and take your money, and return to the residence, give the card back and nobody says a thing. Everyone knows they will come back next week and do the same thing until the offender's day is done.

Smoke, drink, billies, abuse, don't forget the pills and snort a line or two.

I listen for sounds … to hear how many people are inside or in the roof, for sometimes they hide there … I notice if doors are open or shut and if the house is clean and tidy. It rarely is. I sit with my back to the wall at the kitchen table so, I can see the kitchen and the lounge together. I look outside the window and out the back door. I can see everything. Behind the microwave is a knife and beside the fridge is a cricket bat. Somewhere else there is a gun.

Pete, you got a smoke, smoke Peter.

Yep, everyone's smoking, making promises. Jessie was picked up from the shopping centre toilets, passed out from chroming. Julie just cannot handle all her children.

She has six as well as other family members, over one hundred in our area.

A notification was put into child protection. That's why I am here.

Child protection.

I knock on the door, and it opens. Julie is there.

Smartly dressed. I look down the corridor.

The house is spotless.

Pause.

Do you know why I am here?

[*As Julie*] Yes, I do.

What would you like to do?

Silence.

[*As Julie*] Let them come and do it, sirens, and all.

Okay.

Julie closes the door. I get in the car, drive down the road, pull over and make the call … In the distance I hear the sirens and I look in the mirror at the baby seat.

[*As Subconscious*] Peter, what's happening, I'm listening. Peter, I'm listening.

I think about the case worker who drove Jessie and Rachel home from their case worker meetings in his new red car. Jessie gave him an address. She said was their uncle's place. He waited, they went in, came out and he dropped them home. When he got back to his office, the police called to say there'd been a robbery with a new red car involved.

He was transferred.

Rachel was an interesting type, she told me I was …

[*As Rachel*] A fat f_ _ _ _ _ _ c_ _ _

Which I was, given the time I was spending in the car, no home cooked meals, junk food, free lunches.

But I wasn't offended.

[*As Rachel*] You hungry Peter, you FFC!

I have a policy of see nothing, hear nothing, say nothing, know everything. I make sure that I detach emotionally from the young. Focus on the issues which impact upon their lives and the best way to plant seeds for their future.

And who are we to judge?

God, Bunjil or whoever we believe in has that right.

And we will be judged ourselves upon our judgement day.

Pause.

Rachel was twelve when she fell pregnant, her boyfriend was in his twenties. By the time she was seventeen she had four children all placed in care. Her man was a real mongrel, but nothing was going to part them. The department wasn't going down that path anyway.

They just hoped he would get caught and go to jail. They tried to send Rachel back to school but were advised she and the school weren't ready for each other … They went ahead and did it anyway.

They did it; they really went ahead and did it.

By the time her first day was over she had told the school bully she would …

[*As Rachel*] Cut off your head; stick a football up your bottom and watch it pop out your headless neck.

By sunset Rachel and Jessie were having a party on the roof with petrol taken from the school's ute. They both had warrants for breach of bail.

Breach of bail.

I go around to their aunties' place to ask them if they want to deal with the warrants. Oddly enough they both say yes …

I notice down the corridor the kitchen table with family members round it smoking cones. Jessie and Rachel come out. We are just about to leave when their grandmother hits me up for some smokes and tells the girls to behave themselves.

They think it was funny. When we get to the police station, I ask for Detective Such-and-Such who takes us to an interview room and asks …

[*As Detective*] Would you like tea or coffee?

Tea please. Black no sugar. Out of courtesy, he asked the girls.

[*As Rachel/Jessie*] Coffee please, six sugars.

We sit there, waiting. That's what you do when you are at the police station: wait. You're not going anywhere when you're at the police station. The girls were giggling and fidgety, I bend down to do up my shoelace and notice them passing something under the table.

What have you got there?

They both pop a pill, the door opens, the detective comes back in, they put six sugars into their coffee and drink it. I sit in court watching two kids off their faces promising, they will abide by yet another court order.

Unbelievable!

The breach of bail was for a robbery at a church.

Our father who aren't in heaven hollow be thy name.

Distract and divert, distract, and divert.

It is a Sunday, and Jessie and Rachel are on a mission. Nearly every church has a residency and when the girls knock on one door, a nun opens it.

[*As Rachel/Jessie*] We have no food at home, Mum sent us here because all the food banks are closed, and our brothers and sisters are hungry, and we was hoping you might be able to help us?

The nun invites them in. When she goes into the kitchen, Jessie asks …

[*As Jessie*] Can I use the phone to let Mum know we're alright and that the church is going to help us?

And the nun says

[*As Nun*] Yes of course, oh dear.

And Rachel says

[*As Rachel*] Can I please use the toilet?

And the nun says

[*As Nun*] Yes of course dear, down the corridor, turn right.

Distract and divert, distract, and divert.

[*As Rachel/Jessie*] Thank you.

While Jessie is on the phone calling her cousins up bush, she positions herself for a view of the nun getting the food together. Rachel goes down the corridor, doesn't turn right but scans the bedrooms for something to steal.

[*As Rachel*] Distract and divert.

Still on the phone Jessie notices a handbag hanging over a chair. One eye on the nun, she opens the bag, finds a wallet and a digital camera, and hangs up as the nun comes back with the food. In the background the toilet flushes and Rachel meets her at the front door.

[*As Rachel/Jessie*] Thank you so much, Mum will be so grateful for the church's generosity.

The door closes and they are off down the street. When they are out of sight, they throw the food into the bin, go through the wallet, take the money, and keep the digital camera. A few hours later the nun realises.

Realises.

Realises she has been robbed, calls the police and fingers Jessie and Rachel from their mugshot. The police pick them up, interview them, get them to empty their pockets and a digital camera appears.

[*As police*] Whose camera is this?
[*As Rachel*] Mine.
Rachel says it's hers.
[*As Jessie*] Mine.
Jessie says it's hers.

The nun confirms it is the one stolen from her bag and the girls are charged with theft. They get bail and a date to appear in court before the magistrate, for which they don't turn up. Hence the breach of bail.

Silence.

I love this place. I love the water and the breeze as it whips in from the ocean. I love the sunrise and the colours which light up the morning sky. I love hearing the crashing of the waves as they hit the shore.

I love my sanctuary and my escape from the world.

Pause.

I love my silence.

II. RAINBOW SERPENT STORY

Shadow moving.

VOICEOVER: In the Creation, a group of men were out hunting Wallabies. It had been raining and the ground was soft, making it hard for them to run. The Wallabies, refreshed by the rain, were flighty and difficult to catch. The men came to a clump of trees near the edge of a small plain and decided to rest. There they sat around telling stories.

Warming his hands by the fire, one of them looked up. On the horizon was a beautiful multicoloured arch. A Rainbow! 'There goes the Rainbow Serpent moving from waterhole to waterhole'. They were a little fearful. They did not want the huge, brightly coloured Serpent near their camp. They were grateful it did not seem to be moving closer.

They talked about hunting and fishing and the battles they had fought. One young man wanted to know more about the Rainbow Serpent. The other hunters laughed. 'Be patient' they said, 'you will find out in time.' But the young man wanted to find out straight away.

When they returned, the children ran out to greet them and even though they had only two Wallabies, not really enough for everyone, there would be singing and dancing and a big Corroboree. The young man waited until given permission to sit with the older men. Then he asked them about the Rainbow Serpent. The old men said it was one of the Creation Creatures who had shaped our mother earth.

In the beginning the earth was flat, a vast grey plain. As the Rainbow Serpent wound his way across the land, the movement of his body heaped up the mountains and dug troughs for the rivers. With each thrust of his huge multicoloured body, a new landform was created. He was the biggest of the Creation Creatures. Even the other Living Ancestors thought he was enormous and were very careful to leave him alone.

At last, tired with the effort of shaping the earth, he crawled into a waterhole. The cool water washed over his vast body, soothing him. The other animals watched as the water blurred the bright colours. Then he sank from sight. Each time the animals visited the waterhole though they could not see him, they knew he was there. Then one day, after a heavy rainstorm, his huge, coloured body arched up over the treetops, through the clouds, and across the plains.

To this day, young men are careful not to disturb the Rainbow Serpent when they see him going across the sky from waterhole to waterhole, forming our rainbows.

THE MAN

Enter PETER.

PETER: One thing that doesn't surprise me are the predators out there, lurking in the shadows for the vulnerable young lost in their desolate world. Some children can't see the light for the darkness. All it takes is one person to change the lives of so many.

[*As Subconscious*] Peter.

When a young person comes into conflict with their family, it usually involves the parent's issues impacting on the child. Children of the First People have so many issues affecting their lives. They see, feel and hear their world differently than travellers who have come to our shores. All it takes is for one person to engage them in drugs and alcohol and a child's spiritual connection is shattered.

Just one person.

And your sanctuary trembles as cracks appear within its foundations.

Cracks appear.

The system arrives into research, interview and conclude it is there to help and support your family. Before you know it, your child is taken and living in a residency.

Your child now has a licence to do whatever the f_ _ _ they want and if something occurs the police are called automatically, it's procedure, they have to call.

Policy and procedure.

Your child now engages with other children who have been removed and come into contact with the justice system. The residencies may not be near each other but there are no secrets. They are now connected to another world, a world where their issues impact upon each other.

Mental health, adolescence, physical, sexual, psychological abuse, anger, violence, suicide, self-harm, chroming, drugs, and alcohol.

You put them into a witch's melting pot and stir them all together and they explode. Windows smashed, new cars damaged. Houses set on fire. Fighting, verbal abuse, threats to kill. The offending begins to escalate.

The police are called. It is automatic.

Policy and procedure. Policy and procedure.

A threat with a plastic fork, police are called, threat to kill. Megan knew the police station inside out. She had lived in the residencies for four years, was diagnosed with many different personalities.

If Megan wasn't taking her medication your day was always an adventure. I remember walking behind her putting back the fence posts she was pulling down.

She drove everyone insane.

[*An echo*] Insane. Insane.

She has no pain threshold. I saw her hurt herself one time. She gave a deadly performance, but I saw no real feelings there at all.

Her mother is a witch.

A child with no love or void of care is looking ... searching, engaging with the one person who without a doubt will change their life in the wrong way forever. She was thirteen, mental issues, he was forty. They ended up at the same program for different reasons. We found out about it through a young offender who said he noticed them holding hands on a bus and followed them home, where allegedly he saw them through a window, naked. A very dangerous scenario. For other members of the community: *Do Not Take Kindly.*

Do Not Take Kindly.

To vampires baying for a virgin's blood. Then this boy called the older man to say he knew what was going on ...

Happy New Year. Happy New Year!

Sounds and lights of New Year's Eve.

This section is delivered as a police report in court.

NOTE: The actor can hold the script from pp. 13–16 to deliver it if they wish.

PETER *puts on a tie and a pair of glasses. Spotlight on* PETER.

Good morning *Your Honour*. It is the night of the thirty-first of December. The man is home alone.

The vampire.

Dozing on the couch in the lounge room of his flat, one in a group of five that share a common driveway. At approximately eleven forty p.m. the boy and a friend drive to the man's address in a black Utility, registration number Da Da Da Da Da Da.

And park the ute in the service road out front.

The boy leaves the vehicle carrying a silver-coloured tyre iron.

His friend remains in the driver's seat.

Your Honour

The boy bangs on the front of the flat and calls out for the man to ...

[*As Andrew*] Open the bloody door.

He repeats this demand several times.

Pause.

The man looks out and sees Andrew standing there holding the tyre iron in his right hand, who then says to him …

[*As Andrew*] Open the bloody door or I'm going to smash the window.

Andrew uses the tyre iron to force open the security door, still yelling at the man to open up. Fearing Andrew would smash his way in, the man opens the front door …

Your Honour, Andrew enters.

He actually enters.

Andrew grabs the man by the shirt and drags him to the ute parked in the street. He is still armed with the tyre iron, so the man doesn't struggle, fearing he will be assaulted. Andrew then has a conversation with his friend, during which the friend gets out of the vehicle and takes possession of the tyre iron from Andrew, who says.

[*As Andrew*] Watch him. Watch him.

Andrew reparks the ute outside the victim's flat. When Andrew alights, he regains the tyre iron and takes the man inside. Andrew tells him to pack up his property as he is taking it. He tells him.

[*As Andrew*] This is for doing a thirteen-year-old girl.

Your Honour.

Andrew and his friend, aided by the man, then carry the following property to the ute:—

One sixty-eight-centimetre television, one DVD player, one surround-sound stereo system, one flat-screen computer monitor, one computer hard drive and one microwave.

Andrew sorts through the man's DVD collection. He places numerous DVDs in plastic bags. A white doona is also taken; Andrew tells the man if he calls the police, *Your Honour*.

He will kill him and then go round to the man's family and kill them too because he knows where they live.

Andrew asks the man for money.

Picking up the man's wallet off the couch.

He removes one hundred and sixty dollars in cash and a bank debit-card number.

Da Da Da Da Da Da Da.

He asks the man for his pin, who writes it down.

Da Da Da Da.

... on a portion of a former bill and hands it to Andrew. Andrew gives his friend two fifty-dollar notes and tells him to buy some alcohol. As he is leaving his friend says.

Don't hurt him.

To which Andrew replies.

[*As Andrew*] Oh, I won't hurt him. I just want to talk to him.

After his friend has left, Andrew picks up a cardboard box and lights a corner of it with a cigarette lighter.

He waves it in front of the man's face and says.

[*As Andrew*] Make a choice, get burned or get bashed.

The man replies, *Your Honour*.

I'd rather get bashed than burned.

Andrew drops the burning box on the floor.

The man puts it out under the tap in the kitchen sink. Andrew then pushes the man into the bathroom at the rear of the flat and commences punching and kicking him in the face, stomach, and chest.

Punch/sound.

The man falls to the floor and covers his face with his arms. Andrew grabs him by the hair and drags him to the toilet where he pushes his head into the bowl, holds it under and flushes it.

Sound of toilet flushing.

Your Honour, Andrew then picks up a green bottle of hospital-grade disinfectant and pours it over the man's head. The liquid runs over his hair and into his eyes. Andrew then pushes the man into the shower, turns on the water and says

Get under and wash yourself off.

When he gets out of the shower, Andrew and his friend are seen leaving from a neighbouring flat.

Andrew calls out.

[*As Andrew*] Happy New Year. Happy New Year.

The man is assisted by witnesses to the hospital where his injuries are treated. Police were then called.

Megan states that she *wasn't* having a sexual relationship.

The man isn't forty years old. He is twenty-one, *Your Honour.*

The vampire ... *My apologies Your Honour*. The man states, that he and Megan were lying on a mattress in his bedroom watching a DVD and fell asleep. Two days later ...

Happy New Year.

Your Honour, the medical examiner finds

Very painful ... 'red eyes—*chemical injury*—swollen tender lip', right-side abdominal, flank and chest tenderness.

Andrew is then charged with aggravated burglary and intentionally causing injury, he tells the police he was on drugs and alcohol that night and heavily affected. Andrew's on drugs and alcohol most nights. His life is filled with trauma. He was once in the top-ten most-wanted people in the city.

But he has accepted responsibility for his actions, *Your Honour*, and accepts your decision.

Two years wholly suspended. Three hundred hours community work with drug and alcohol counselling.

Thank you, *Your Honour*.

Spotlight slowly fades on chair.

PETER *takes off the tie and glasses.*

PETER *goes back to his sanctuary.*

Spotlight up on PETER.

I love this place. I love the water and the breeze as it whips in from the ocean.

Pause.

I love my sanctuary, my escape from the world.

III. THE SUN WOMAN, THE FIRST SUNRISE

Shadow moving.

VOICEOVER: Long ago before creation, the earth was very dark. A grey blanket of clouds kept the light and the warmth out. It was very cold and very black. This great grey mass of cloud was so low the animals had to crawl around. The Emu hobbled; neck bent almost to the ground. The Kangaroo couldn't hop, and none of the birds could fly higher than a few feet. Only the snakes were happy because they lived close to the ground.

The Animals lived by crawling around the damp earth feeling for fruits and berries. Often it was hard to find food and several days would pass between meals. The Wombat became so tired of people bumping into him that he dug himself a burrow and learned to sleep for long periods.

Eventually, the birds decided they'd had enough. They called a meeting of all the animals. The Magpies, who were more intelligent than most birds, had a plan: 'We can't fly because the sky is too low. What we need to do is raise it. If we all gathered sticks, we could use them to push the sky up and we could fly up with the sky and make lots of room for everyone.'

All the animals agreed it was a good plan and set about gathering sticks. The Magpies took a big stick each and began to push at the sky. 'Look, it's going to work! The sky! It's moving!' The Emus and the Kangaroos, the Wombats and the Goannas watched as the Magpies pushed the sky slowly upwards. They used sticks as levers, first resting the sky on low boulders, then on small hills.

The animals watched the Magpies pushing and straining until they finally reached the top of a mountain. They gave mighty cheer, and all said, 'at least we can now walk about.' The Emu and the Kangaroo moved in long proud hops. But it was still very dark. The Magpies kept pushing the sky higher and higher until they reached the highest mountain in the land.

Then with a mighty heave, they gave the sky one last push! The sky shot up into the air and as it rose it split open and a huge flood of warmth and light poured onto the land below. The animals were in awe of the light and warmth, but more so at the incredible brightly painted beauty of the Sun-Woman. The whole sky was awash with beautiful reds and yellows ... *It was the first Sunrise.*

Overjoyed with the light and the warmth, the magpies burst into song. As their loud warbling carried across the land, the Sun-Woman rose slowly and began her journey towards the West. Now each morning when the Sun-Woman wakes in her camp in the East, she lights a fire and prepares the bark torch she will carry across the sky each day. It is this fire that provides the first light of dawn.

As she puts on her paint, the dust from the crushed red ochre colours the early morning clouds a beautiful soft red. Then she takes up her flaming bark torch. When she reaches the Western edge of the world she sits down, repaints herself, ready for her journey through a long underground passage, back to her camp in the East.

That is why, to this day, every morning when the Sun-Woman wakes, and lights her early morning fire, all the Magpies greet her with their beautiful song.

ANDREW'S STORY

Enter PETER.

PETER: When I came back to this place from another place there was nothing here and everybody was going nowhere. I wrote not like Shakespeare, and I wrote, not like Austen and I wrote, not like Birch but we pushed the boundaries and created something special.

I was told not to reinvent the wheel and I didn't. I just learnt to understand the wheel really well.

Really well.

I reported to a supervisor once a year, the operation manager would lend me their ear and through union we were able to plant seeds. I saw us as gardeners. We would plant seeds that would grow a strong tree with healthy branches. But when you walk a fine line between life and death sometimes healthy doesn't come into it. Half the time the seeds wouldn't have had a feed, or the chance to change their socks. Some of them homeless, some of them in residencies, some of them couch-surfing, all of them surviving day to day. The system makes it easy.

Use the system. Present the apple. Use the system.

When they turn a certain age, if they are not living at home they go onto welfare payments, every fortnight. It all goes on drugs and alcohol. Then for the other thirteen days they have nothing.

Surviving, day to day, day to day, surviving.

The system gives them money, it opens the door. Parents are furious because everybody knows everybody. So, some good kids leave home to get the money and engage with other kids and need more money and so the first rung of the offending begins. They come into contact with the police, the police ring their parents, the kid says they're sorry and the police let them go.

With a warning.

But the arguments continue between the parents and the kid, and the kid takes off again, catches up with their friends and the pattern continues. This happened to Lynne. She was a good kid, but her offending escalated to the point where she was charged with burglary and firearms possession. A gun with a silencer … She was fifteen years old. I thought …

Where the f_ _ _ did you get that?

We ran the program twenty-four seven. Seven days a week and the phone didn't stop.

Phone rings.

This is Senior Constable Such-and-Such we have Joe Da Da Da down at the station, he's been bought in for …

Theft. Joe was an interesting character. You have to watch the quiet types. They say they want to engage and then they don't and then you go to where they live with their mother and they sweet talk you into believing their bullshit. And then they disappear again, and you get another phone call.

Phone rings.

This is Senior Sergeant Such-and-Such we have Joe Da Da Da in at the station and he has been brought in for …

Rape!

Quiet as a mouse he was. His lawyer wanted me to speak at his trial, I hung up the phone. Those girls, perhaps I let them down by not noticing the signs. But I couldn't find him most of the time. Joe got

Six years.

And the girls got life.

Phone rings.

[*As Mary*] It's Mary, I just saw Andrew, he's in trouble and he's carrying something under his jacket.

Where is he?

[*As Mary*] Out the front of the performing arts centre.

Beat.

Near the city mall.

Beat.

Down by the primary school.

Beat.

Up by the railway station.

I'm looking here and I'm looking there, and I get another call Where is he?

[*As Mary*] Out the back yard.

I don't know what to expect so I'm

Cautious. Cautious.

There he is … behind the wheel of a car.

Where are you going?

I say. He doesn't answer. He is focused on his driving.

Andrew.

He moves his hand up and hugs his jacket tightly as if he is hiding something.

Where are you going, mate?

I say again. Andrew shifts in his seat.

Are you alright?

Andrew slowly turns and looks at me. His mouth is a ring of blue, like a blue ringed octopus.

He shifts again, still holding his jacket.

Can I come too?

I get in the passenger side of the car.

Cautiously. Cautiously.

I have walked into a back yard and am sitting in an old sedan on blocks. No wheels, no doors, no passenger seat. I'm looking at Andrew behind the wheel as if he is actually driving this car somewhere. I see him shift in his seat and pull his jacket closer.

So, I'm cautious.

He thinks he is travelling *fast* like in the Grand Prix. My voice is just a blur in his head. When I sit in the car, he holds his jacket as if he has the crown jewels, I say …

Where are you going mate?

He says

[*As Andrew*] Nowhere.

Beat.

Nowhere.

Can I come?
[*As Andrew*] Sure.
Are you okay?
[*As Andrew*] Sure.
What's in your jacket?
[*As Andrew*] Nothing.
Can I have a look?

Andrew opens up his jacket and there are paint spray cans in a plastic bag.

Can I hold it?

Andrew passes me the bag. He trusts me, seriously trusts me. And that is so hard to earn.

Would you like me to take you to the hospital?

I help him into my car and drive him to the hospital.

On the way he lights a cigarette.

[*As Subconscious*] He what?

He lights a cigarette.

You better not do that mate. You have just been chroming and your throat and lungs might (y'know) … *Explode.*

And he looks at me and I look at him and so we both have a cigarette on the way to the hospital.

[*As Subconscious*] Oh Peter.

We get to emergency, and I speak to the front desk, they put us in a side room and a doctor comes to see him. She is very nice, and Andrew sparks up a bit. She has a chat with us, admits him and puts him in a bed. But when Andrew has tubes inserted into him, he gets agitated and the doctor tries to calm him down and security is called and stands outside Andrew's bed and Andrew starts to threaten the guard and the doctor wants to call the psychologist, but Andrew doesn't want to see the psychologist and when the doctor makes the phone call anyway, Andrew says

[*As Andrew*] I'll smash his face in.

And Andrew says

[*As Andrew*] If that bitch calls the psychologist, I'm going to go nuts.

And Andrew says …

[*As Andrew*] Help me out, will you?

And I sit there watching Andrew, watching Andrew watching the security guard, and keeping my one eye on the doctor all at the same time. I monitor Andrew's rhythm. People have an inner rhythm, and it can go from one to ten really quickly, so, you can see the gear changes and whether …

People are in control of them.

Control … total control.

It fires really quickly one to ten, so trying to keep calm and alert is really a test of character and patience.

And did Andrew pass?

No, he failed miserably. He kept saying …

[*As Andrew*] Help me. Help me.

And to the security guard

[*As Andrew*] I will smash you in the face. I'm not scared of you.

And the security guard just stood there. Stood there, watching.

And when Andrew started pulling those tubes from his arm and blood spurted everywhere, he was saying.

[*As Andrew*] Help me.

I went.

No.

I'm not helping you take those things out of your arm,

No. No.

You have to calm down

No. No. No.

Let the doctors do their thing … I need a smoke.

[*As Andrew*] If they call the psychologist.

It might be a good thing.

[*As Andrew*] What.

Andrew is more alert after they give him black tar and have him throwing up. The doctor calls the psychologist.

He is from the psychiatric hospital next door.

I know him well.

[*As Andrew*] You been there?

My sister had … drugs really f_ _ _ you up … she'd come back here from another place and her marriage broke up. She was a good wife but got caught up in pokies shite and lost a lot of money.

Unfortunately, her ex didn't know she had filched the funds until they were going through the divorce. Then she met the wrong person, and they introduced her to hard drugs, and she was hooked. She lost her children, lost everything and sunk deep into the dark world of misery, but she didn't give a f_ _ _. She came home and for three years tormented my soul. My sister, the one who kept me safe. When we heard the footsteps coming down the corridor, she would grab my hand and we would hide under the bed. I tried so hard to support her through this fractured world she had become accustomed to, I understood the bullshit she would talk and the constant paranoia. I felt sorry for her third child, a son to another fella, him caught up in drugs too. Him sitting in prison, her dragging his baby around. The kid nearly drowned in the bath. The family disowned her after that, and she fell.

Fell hard.

Drugs always catch up with you.

You can't escape from them.

And no-one can help you until it's time, time when your body says …

Enough. Enough is enough.

Until that time people will just crap on and exploit the system and say …

Yes.

When they really mean. No.

It's like running around after a headless chook. It burns you out. You get burnt out with the bullshit.

How can you bullshit a bullshitter when the bullshitter bullshits you.

She was a nightmare to be around, talking all the time and fast [*An echo*] Fast. Fast. Fast.

And paranoid about her ex. Not her ex.

But her ex.

The new ex.

Not the ex-ex.

Paranoid he was living in her roof. She couldn't sleep and was scratching herself and the junkies up the road wanted to kill her.

Owed them money probably.

She smashed all her windows and just went nuts. I had to call the police and she resisted, and they placed her in a straitjacket, and she ended up where Andrew's psychologist had come from.

The psychologist.

He's great and he speaks to Andrew, and we go outside and have a smoke.

[*As Subconscious*] A smoke.

And Andrew is fine, sitting outside.

[*As Subconscious*] Outside.

Yes.

[*As Subconscious*] He didn't run away.

No.

The psychologist is good, very good.

I watch him work his magic and he gets Andrew sorted.

We go back into emergency and Andrew is released.

As we are walking out, I say ...

Hey! Haven't you got something to say to the doctor?

Andrew looks at me and I stare back.

[*As Andrew*] What?

Andrew hesitates but he does it.

[*As Andrew*] I'm sorry.

And we walk out. He goes home and smokes billies and drinks bourbon and cokes. I go back to work.

I was on call.

Phone rings.

I ... love ... this ... place ... I ... love my ...

Pause.

... Silence.

IV. KOALA AND THE KANGAROO

Shadow moving.

VOICEOVER: In the Creation, all Koalas had tails. Long ago was the worst drought ever known. Koala and Kangaroo were so thirsty. 'I shall die of thirst,' said Koala, 'I know and I'm bigger than you, so I need more,' said Roo. 'The sky has forgotten to rain,' cried Koala. Roo got angry. 'We should be ashamed to sit down and weep like children. We are warriors! Listen. In the hills there is a dry riverbed. If we went there, we could dig a small waterhole and save ourselves.'

'Come on then,' said Koala and off they went. On the way they saw that all the other birds and animals were in much the same condition as them. Finally, after walking a long time, they made it to the riverbed. Koala decided to trick Roo (for he was lazy). 'Begin for me Roo, for I'm tired. I will help you later,' and he curled up and went to sleep.

Kind Roo had no reason to doubt his friend, so he began to dig in the riverbed with his powerful clawed feet. After a long time, Roo climbed out of the hole, but Koala said …

'The Sun has burnt all the life out of me, I'm sick and I'm surely about to die.'

Without a word, Roo hopped back into the hole and dug even harder to save his friend lying under the tree.

Soon Roo had found the water and was just about to drink when greedy Koala rushed past him (knocking him down) and started to drink the water himself. Roo had been tricked and was very angry. He took a stone knife from his pouch, raised it above his head and brought it down with all his might.

Koala let out a scream and was so scared that he jumped up into the first Gum Tree he could reach. Koala looked down to see Roo with his stone knife in one paw and Koala's tail in the other.

'You are not nice, and you are greedy, and for that you have lost your tail. You do not share, and you are selfish. We are now enemies for all time.' And Koala has been up in the trees ever since, too scared to come down, in case Roo is there, just like he was in the Creation.

PETER'S STORY

Enter PETER.

PETER: My daughter is eight and she has depression.
My son is five and he is angry with me.
[*As Subconscious*] I miss my dad.
My daughter does not want to get out of bed and go to school, my son kicks, punches and raises his voice.
I want to protect them.
Protect them from what?
Their mother is frustrated that her children are suffering because their father is not there.
[*As Subconscious*] Oh Peter.
I want to see my way through this mist, but I can't.
My daughter is in pain and my son is angry and their mother is sad, but they are safe.
Safe …
Safe from the torment of the world, safe from the worms who slither through the streets.
Safe from the prying eyes of the wicked.
[*As Subconscious*] Peter.
What about love? What about love.
Love is a four-letter word taken out of context. I didn't experience it growing up, I never got it from my mother, I never got it from my father, I never got a birthday card or a birthday party, I never had someone read me a book and whisper in my ear as I was falling to sleep, that I love you.
I got the system … The system.
The system never tells you that it loves you, the system doesn't read a book at night, except at the police station when it reads you your rights, the system is based on policy and procedures implemented over one hundred years ago, internal solidarity clauses and once a policy is adopted its representatives are expected to adhere to it, are bound to support every decision. And how can you change policy unless you are within policy, even though policy is not going to change and that means …

There's no love there.

A few decades back, people in our community started to understand the value of the dollar.

There was once a saying that …

Community is unity.

But I think it got lost.

Once the value of the dollar got understood, the unity in community started to crumble.

And when I got back there was nothing here, no strategy, no vision, no program.

Just as I found my voice, they took my voice away.

We cannot let this happen again.

Keep going. Stay strong. Keep going.

I was only there because he let me be there.

The power of one who makes all the decisions is the power of one who controls your destiny …

The power of language …

Apparently, we are no longer Aboriginal.

Suddenly we are now Indigenous, First Nations, another escape route from the past. What about the fraudsters pretending.

What a fool are we to be fooled by fools?

[*As Subconscious*] Peter. Peter.

Okay. Fine.

Five years' work, over four hundred young people, twenty-four hours a day, seven days a week, one full time program, one ten-day camp around the boundaries of country which provided them a knowledge base and connected them to their identity, place and belonging, their role and responsibility in community and how to transform them for the society in which we live.

Years of hard work down the drain.

But it's not going to stop until Mother Nature says it's time. And while society keeps moving forward, we have to continue struggling to get our true voice heard.

We are the gate way to the old world.

We are the connection to the old world.

He gestures.

For I am me and you are you.

He gestures.

For I am me and you are you.

He gestures.

For I am you and you are me.

He gestures.

For I am you and you are me.
Aboriginal.
Australian.

NOTE: If you would like to include your language group, please do.

Silence.

When they come into contact with the Justice system and are placed on a court order they come to me. Twenty-four seven. When they are still sleeping … I whisper in their ear,

Wake up. Get up.

And though they have gone to bed at five a.m.

Drunk, stoned, popping pills, they get up and engage because they want to connect with who they are and who they trust.

Trust.

But if there's no money, there is no tomorrow.

If the system calls it a pilot, you have an in, but they have an out. What now?

Phone rings.

I am asleep but my eyes are open.

I hear the phone ringing in my head, and I say hello.

[*As Subconscious*] Help.

I hear the breath of a desperate soul and my heart is racing.

[*As Subconscious*] Help.

I wonder if I am dreaming.

[*As Subconscious*] Help.

The sounds are panicky.

[*As Subconscious*] Help me.

Yes.

[*As Subconscious*] Help me.

Yes. Yes. I'm here. Wake up Peter. Wake up Peter.
[*As Subconscious*] You're dreaming.
No.
[*As Subconscious*] Help me!
Yes.
[*As Subconscious*] Wake up Peter.
I am here … I see you.
[*As Subconscious*] Do you?
Yes.
[*As Subconscious*] Peter. Peter.
I see you … hanging from a tree.

Phone rings.

Hello?

Silence.

Hello?

Silence.

Hello?

Silence.

I am sitting in a pub when I hear a voice say …
[*As Young Voice*] Hello Peter
He was a young man.
I don't recognise him, but I play along, and he introduces me to his mother and his girlfriend.
[*As Mother*] Hello
[*As Girlfriend*] Hello
And he says
[*As Young Voice*] Do you recognise me?
I look at him but still can't place him.
[*As Young Voice*] I am from the place where you have just been.
And I stare at him, and his mother says …
[*As Mother*] I want to thank you for changing my son's life.
And the boy had become a man
and he shakes my hand.
[*As Young Voice*] You changed my life.
You're welcome.

Silence.

I will get up in the morning and I will go to the phone.
    I will get up in the morning and I will dress myself.
    I will get up in the morning and I will go to work.
    I will get up in the morning.
    I will be up in the evening, and I will wait for the phone.
    I will be up in the evening, and I will be dressed.
    I will be up in the evening and will wait.
    I will be up in the evening.
    I will be up in the night and answer the phone.
    I will be up in the night fully dressed.
    I will be up in the night and respond.
    I will be up in the night and gone.
    I will be up in the night and gone.

EPILOGUE

Low energy, static rumbling, distorted ocean, wind.
Shadows talking. Enter PETER.

PETER: Father ... There is an old man with long grey hair and beard. He is as old as the beginning of time, every morning he stands on the edge of the water waiting for the sun to rise. He listens to the sounds which surround him and sees three magpies perched in a tree.
   They sing the songs of the new dawn approaching.
   [*Spoken softly, there is a rhythm here*] I can see the sun rising on the shore.
   I can feel its power knocking on our door.
   I can hear its whispers as the dawn begins to rise.
   I can see its beauty in the light of my clear eyes.
   I am here.
   You are there.
   When we meet.
   Know I care.
   I can see my son standing on the shore.
   I can feel his presence knocking on my door.
   I can hear his whispers as the dawn begins to rise.
   I can see my daughter and the beauty in her eyes.
   I am here.
   You are there.
   When we meet.
   Know I care.
   I can see the sun rising on the shore.
   I can feel its power knocking on our door.
   I can hear its whispers as the dawn begins to rise.
   I can see its beauty in the light of my clear eyes.
   I am here.
   You are there.
   When we meet.
   Know I care.
   Silence.

He feels the wind as it touches the tip of his fingers, and he watches the breeze as it dances with the leaves in the tree.

He understands the rhythms of the day from this ritual that he performs every morning.

He watches the horizon and sees the warrior ancestors protecting the gateway to the spirit world.

Many of our people are there, many won't make it.

He watches the streak of light as it touches Mother Earth for the first time and wonders how many lost souls know this feeling.

He listens to the water as the ripples sing their songs, and he hears the animals as they yawn away the night.

He sees the moon faint in the distance and thinks of the achievements of man.

Yet here he is alone again on the edge of the shore on a new day, he has waited so long for the lost to arise.

The sun rises to warm the world.

A cold chill engulfs the dead as they sleep away the day from the devils dancing in the night …

while three magpies perched in a tree watch on.

The new day is here.

PETER *watches and listens.*

Lights fade to black.

Shadows lightly talking.

THE END

presents

Three Magpies Perched in a Tree

Written by Glenn Shea

Peter: Glenn Shea
Creation Story Voiceovers: Uncle Jack Charles
Director: Glenn Shea
Associate Director: Dr. Kirsty M Reilly
Set Designer: Meg White
Lighting Designer: Bronwyn Pringle
Sound Designer: Elissa Goodrich
Stage Manager: Kelly Harris
Assistant Stage Manager: Tess Nethercote – Way
Social Media / Marketing: Lucy Payne
Animation 2D: Mia-Bijou Gollan Reilly-Shea

La Mama Courthouse
14–25 August, 2024

CREATOR'S ACKNOWLEDGEMENTS

I would like to thank Dr Kirsty M Reilly the mother of my children Mia and Finn for all the pain and suffering caused by having a loved one and a father work within a justice system that is so fractured and traumatic that it impacts on the lives of those you love and who are closest to you in your everyday walk of life.

I would also like to thank Professor Julian Meyrick, the wonderful Judith Sears, your constant support has never wavered, I would like to thank Liz Jones, Adam Cass and Caitlin Dullard from La Mama Theatre, they provided me the opportunity to co-produce and present *Three Magpies Perched in a Tree* as part of An Indigenous Trilogy at the courthouse Theatre, Melbourne.

I would like to thank the Wathaurong Aboriginal Community/Cooperative. I am so pleased to present these true stories to our elders and community in a proper way.

To Maureen Hartley, La Mama, thank you for your wisdom and support through this process.

And finally, the team at Currency Press for their assistance with the publication of this book.

AWARDS

Three Magpies Perched in a Tree has received the following awards:
State Library of Victoria R.E Ross Trust Development Award 2010
Playwriting Australia Script Workshop Selection Award 2010
City of Greater Geelong Professional Development Award 2010
World Theatre Festival Presentation Reading 2011
Playwriting Australia National Script Workshops 2011
State Library of Victoria – Flash Point Reading 2011
Victoria's Premier Literacy Awards 2023 HIGHLY COMMENDED
Green Room Award Independent Best New Writing 2023:
Act 1: *Three Magpies Perched in a Tree: An Indigenous Trilogy*

This printed version of *Three Magpies Perched in a Tree* has changed from a four-character play to a one person show.

WRITER'S NOTES

The first conversation I had regarding this story was with Professor Julian Meyrick. He was directing *The Birthday Party* by Harold Pinter and had cast me in the role of McCann. I was working as a frontline Aboriginal juvenile justice worker and had engaged in so many issues impacting with our young people and community over decades without proper debriefing or counselling support. Because of this, *The Birthday Party* was impacting me, so I spoke to Julian about all these stories in my head. Julian suggested I write a story about them and give him a copy of the stories at the end of the season, closing night, which I did. I think he was a bit taken back by the fact I actually provided him with a script—we were performing in the Fairfax studio of the Arts Centre (Melbourne) with matiness and evening performances but during the day, I would go into a dressing room and I would quietly write before anybody came in, and then when the two hour call came, I began my process for the matinee or evening performance. Julian then worked with me on the story which became a script and *Three Magpies Perched in a Tree* was born with four characters.

We provided a presentation / reading to the Wathaurong Aboriginal Community on 7 December 2012, with the following cast and creatives:

Producer: THE STORYTELLER® Glenn Shea
Creative Producer: Judith Sears
Project Manager: Sheenagh Mulroy
Director / Dramaturgy: Professor Julian Meyrick
Writer: Glenn Shea
Assistant Director: Kirsty Reilly
Production Manager: Jessica Wong
Stage Manager: Erin Padbury
Wathaurong Community Mentorship: Dean Hollander

Peter, Glenn Shea
Peta, Lisa Maza
Peter 2, Luke Elliott
Hope & Ballerina Dancer, Jessica Lesosky

DIRECTOR'S NOTES

I love what I do—creating human storytelling magnified. Whether on stage, film, a canvas, or written, I offer audiences a chance to see themselves reflected as we navigate the enigma of Life.

I am fortunate to have been part of the evolution of *Three Magpies Perched in a Tree* since its beginnings in 2012. My approach has been to support and guide the actor to reveal the myriad of layers, voices, and worlds within the stories, capturing the powerful subtlety beneath the chaos of Peter's experiences. The writer challenges the director to balance the timeless Creation stories with the damaged, fractured daily life-reality of the Aboriginal youth and the worker. Here are two disparate worlds in time and place. The writing, though seemingly simple holds a plethora of metaphor, poetic truth telling, cultural knowledge and society's systemic underbelly.

So, as a director, I stepped back and listened … deeply. Being culturally aligned and competent ensured the integrity of the story was maintained. Harmonious meeting points were explored between Western and Indigenous theatre processes to find the unique language and understanding required to do the play justice. As an acute observer of all that is felt and unsaid, I utilised this skill to help the actor tap into their deep inner life and bring forward the truth of things. This highlighted the beauty and grace found in dark places. It allowed the humanity of Peter and those he speaks of to shine through, driving the story.

Dr Kirsty M Reilly

DESIGNER'S NOTES

Three Magpies Perched in a Tree is a highly descriptive text. When we read, or hear, Peter's words spoken, and the stories of creation, a myriad of times, places, and stories are elucidated for us. The beautiful and the traumatic are both richly and poetically detailed. If you close your eyes and listen, you will see. Peter is there, opening a door to his world(s), inviting us on a journey.

The design process respects Peter's generous invitation. It engages with the physical places and emotional heart within each story. Concepts, phrases, and key words are unpacked and explored. Hand sketches create a fluid story board capturing these moments of beauty, timelessness, despair, pain, and hope. This story board then supports discussion and further insight between the writer, directors, actor, and creative team. The design acknowledges the poetry and generosity at the core of the writing. It aims to evoke multiple, nuanced, readings. There is not one place. There is not one story or one theme. There are many. The abstraction of elements, places, textures, and times will encourage multivalent readings. As the play unfolds, perceptions of the design elements will unfold too.

Meg White

LIGHTING DESIGNER'S NOTES

One of the first conversations I had with Glenn about this play was about the importance of sitting around a fire having a yarn. That image was key to the first season and remains firmly in my mind. It's a common misconception that lighting design in performance started once we had movable electric fixtures, when actually, light has been part of storytelling for for thousands of years. The fire creates a focal point to gather, the movement of the fire makes the shadows dance, the brightness of the fire makes everything beyond the reach of the fire's glow fade away. I want to feel the echoes of this as we sit in the theatre.

This design has been on a journey. Every time an element changes, the design shifts to make room for new ideas. The first season needed the flexibility to create two shows within the same lighting rig. As I write, we are approaching a new season with some new collaborators who will bring new ideas that will shift things again. Live performance is nimble and shifts a little in every performance. It will be different as you watch it to where my thoughts are now. Enjoy the ride.

Bronwyn Pringle

SOUND DESIGNER'S NOTES

In considering the sound design and original music composition for *Three Magpies Perched in a Tree* I listen deeply to this story and its contexts, contemporary and spiritual. I listen for the language, spoken, sung, for the melodies, the cadences, the rhythms, and the shifting pulse of the work, the fragmented cacophony of humans in strife and the power and beauty of nature's callings. I find ways to honour these, a soundscape for the two worlds Peter straddles. To honour his voice, his story, his uniquely layered experiences of worlds. I wanted to also create soundscapes that honour the voices of the Aboriginal youth that haunt him and the jarring dichotomy between fractured, violent contemporary worlds and the spiritual, poetic, mythic, natural world that co-exist. Sound locates us immediately in time and place. I aimed to create a sonic presence enabling us to hear, feel, and, at times to be in both places at once, and to support the play's (Peter's) back and forth between the two worlds. I wanted the music and sound to reveal itself slowly, asking us listener-audiences to take time, to listen deeply, to hear the precious silences and the presence of beauty and compassion, even in the greatest of turbulence.

Elissa Goodrich

UNCLE GLENN SHEA
Elder / Respected Person NAIDOC 2020 Wathaurong

Producer / Writer / Director / Actor / Cultural Facilitator / Inventor / First Nations Producer La Mama Theatre

Glenn is a proud Wathaurong/Ngarrindjeri man and recent recipient of the 2020 NAIDOC Award for Elder and Respected Person Wathaurong Aboriginal Cooperative for outstanding cultural/program service to community. Winner 2023 Green Room Award for Best New Writing, *Three Magpies Perched in a Tree, An Indigenous Trilogy*. Glenn is a former Research Fellow, Indigenous Creative within School of Humanities & Social Science, Faculty of Arts and Education at Deakin University. Glenn was the first Aboriginal person to graduate from NIDA with a degree in Dramatic Art. A former frontline Koorie youth justice worker. A Board Director of Ilbijerri and Wathaurong. Glenn is the very first, First Nations producer La Mama Theatre Melbourne. Researcher/Curator History of Blak Theatre 1967-2000 Exhibition Powerhouse Museum Sydney. MC Adelaide Festival. MC Dreamtime @ the G Presidents Dinner Essendon versus Richmond AFL.

PROFESSOR JULIAN MEYRICK
Dramaturg

Julian is Professor of Creative Arts at Griffith University and Literary Adviser for the Queensland Theatre. He was Associate Director and Literary Advisor at Melbourne Theatre Company 2002-07 and Artistic Director of kickhouse theatre 1989-98. He was the developing director of Glenn's *Three Magpies Perched in a Tree*, and later for *MI:WI 3027*. He has directed over 40 award-winning theatre productions, written the histories of five Australian theatre companies, and published numerous articles on Australian arts and culture, including 90+ pieces for *The Conversation*. His latest books, *Australia in 50 Plays* and *Theatre and Australia*, were published by Currency Press in 2022 and Bloomsbury in 2024 respectively.

DR KIRSTY M REILLY
Associate Director

A Deakin University(B.Ed), NIDA graduate and Gloria Payton Fellowship recipient, Kirsty trained internationally and worked with Theatre de Complicite, Monica Pagneux, Philippe Gaulier, Sydney Dance Company and DV8. She holds a PhD in Intercultural Alliance and Communication in theatre rehearsal practice, specialising in Intercultural Australian First Nation's theatre making. Professional experience: NIDA and NIDA Corporate (34 yrs ongoing), The Conservatoire of Scotland, Melbourne University (VCA), Actors Centre Australia, 16th Street Actors Studio, and theatre companies including MTC, STC, Opera Australia, Griffin Theatre Sydney, Belvoir St Theatre Sydney, and La Mama theatre Melbourne. Mother to two Wathaurong/Ngarrindjeri children.

MEG WHITE
Designer

Meg has worked in theatre for over 35 years, primarily as a designer. Some of her more recent work includes MI:WI 3027 (Design, La Mama), Hallowed Ground (Design, La Mama), Aphanisis (Performer, La Mama) Madness of the Day (Design, La Mama). Meg has been nominated for and been awarded several Green Room awards in the field of design. Nominations include Body of Work (1999); Krapp's Last Tape; Paradise and Poet #7. Awards include Bauernhof and Mr Puntila and his man Matti. Meg also practices as an architect. She was recently the design architect for Re-build La Mama, which was shortlisted in the Victorian Architecture Awards 2022. Meg exhibited and presented the design process of the rebuild at Prague Quadrennial 2023 as part of the Performance Space Exhibition.

BRONWYN PRINGLE
Lighting Designer

Bronwyn first stepped into La Mama as a performer in 1993. Since then, she turned her attention to lighting design and has worked around Australia and the world in venues ranging from The Princess Theatre, a London West-End Nightclub, a warehouse in Buenos Aires, the Federation Square air-conditioning ducts, and a woolshed in Glencoe, but La Mama remains a special place for experimentation and storytelling. Design highlights from over 80 productions at La Mama include Yarn, Closed for Maintenance, Aviary, Beneath and Beyond and Songbirds and Angels. Bronwyn received the 2020 Green Room Award for Technical Achievement plus three Green Room Awards for Lighting design, including for alias Grace (Malthouse Theatre 2004) which began as her first design in La Mama in 1999.

ELISSA GOODRICH
Sound Designer

Composer/sound artist/percussionist Elissa's works play in festivals across Europe, North America, and Australasia. Elissa's original music intersects contemporary jazz and classical idioms. Multi-award winner for her compositions include co-nominee for 2x APRA_AMCOS *Australian Jazz Work of the Year* with Clare Shannon (*Shannon-Goodrich Ensemble*), 4x Green Room Awards including "Outstanding Composition and Sound Design", and "Production" for Elissa's *Gene Tree Listen Now Again* (with St Martins YPAC and Royal Botanic Gardens Vic). Since 2015 Elissa's practice includes collaborating at the intersections of climate science and new music: *The Waves Project* continues with *Surf Sounds* (Swinburne/Melbourne University).

KELLY HARRIS
Stage Manager

Kelly (Production / Stage Manager) has been working with Glenn Shea over the past 2 years, on such works as; *MI:WI 3027 by Glenn Shea* (2023) and *An Indigenous Trilogy by Glenn Shea* (2022). She is also very excited to join the team for the upcoming season of *Three Magpies Perched in a Tree* (2024). With a B.A in Theatre (from La Trobe Uni), Kelly has worked on *The Marriage of Figaro* (Melbourne Opera) and most recently as a Production/Stage Manager for *The Crucible* (The Australian Shakespeare Company). Kelly loves thought-provoking theatre and loves working with Glenn, helping to bring his beautiful writing come to life.

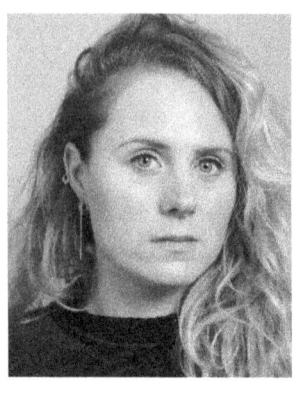 

TESS NETHERCOT –WAY
Assistant Stage Manager / Theatre Maker

Tess is a theatre maker, producer and performer who creates interdisciplinary performance work-based in devising processes. A graduate of Deakin University's Bachelor of Creative Arts majoring in Drama, Tess is interested in upending traditional theatrical conventions to create bold, dynamic, and relevant theatre, driven by curiosity and a commitment to artistic collaboration and connection. Her production credits include assistant stage manager on *MI:WI 3027* (LaMama) and producer on *Sneaky Little Bugger* (La Mama). Tess is thrilled to be a part of the creative team, working for a second time with Glenn Shea as assistant stage manager on *Three Magpies Perched in a Tree*.

LUCY PAYNE
Social Media / Marketing / Actor / Intimacy Coordinator

Lucy is a queer artist based in Naarm/Melbourne. As a performer her theatre credits include *Unestablished*, *MI:WI 3027* and *An Indigenous Trilogy* (La Mama), *Exiles* (Forty-Five-Downstairs), *Bayou Bart* (Theatreworks), *Hey is Dee Dee Home?* (The Knack Theatre) and *The Crucible*, *Brontë* and *Everyman* for BAPA. Alongside acting Lucy also works as a director, producer, facilitator, and designer and is currently working towards accreditation as an Intimacy Director with Intimacy Directors & Coordinators International. Her creative credits include productions for Theatreworks, La Mama, The Butterfly Club, Victorian Theatre Company, and multiple independent works. Lucy was part of the 2023 La Mama Pathways course for emerging playwrights. She is a proud MEAA member.

MIA-BIJOU GOLLAN REILLY-SHEA
Wathaurong/Ngarrindjeri
Animation / 2D

Mia's understanding of how to draw and love of animation comes from the very early designs of Walt Disney and how his imagination and vision inspired the creation of Micky Mouse and Friends. Mia travelled to Disneyland and lived in New York in consultation with her animation associates. Mia has worked on *An Indigenous Trilogy* 2022, *MI:WI 3027* 2023 and *Three Magpies Perched in a Tree* 2024. Mia also designs for THE STORYTELLER® Indigenous Learning and has animated the creation stories, Creation, Rainbow Serpent, First Sunrise and Koala and the Kangaroo. Mia has also been a cultural support facilitator engaging with Melbourne Girls' Grammar and Trinity Grammar. Mia continues to study and develop her skills so that one day she may work for Disney Animation. Her images are Published on THE STORYTELLER® You Tube Channel: https://youtube.com/playlist?list=PLIPF3dInBorfdxvRGW9OZx8d9-Zwqw1p_&si=0CwuZXugTl5SXMX0

CEO & Director – Caitlin Dullard
Marketing and Communications Manager – Georgina Capper
Development & Pathways Manager – Myf Powell
Venue Technical Manager – Hayley Fox
Acting Venue Technical Manager – Shane Grant
Producer – Amber Hart
First Nations Producer/ Curator – Glenn Shea
Learning Producer & School Publications Coordinator – Maureen Hartley
Ticketing & FOH Supervisors – AYA & Gemma Horbury
Design & Marketing Admin – Adam Cass
On-line Producer – Ruiqi Fu

Curators: Gemma Horbury (**Musica**); Amanda Anastasi (**Poetica**); Isabel Knight (**Cabaretica**); Sophia Constantine (**La Mama for Kids**); Emma Fawcett (**La Mama Scratch**)
Documentation – Darren Gill

COMMITTEE OF MANAGEMENT: Helen Hopkins (Chair), Caroline Lee (Deputy Chair), Ben Grant (Treasurer), Caitlin Dullard (Secretary), **Members:** Angela Buckingham, David Geoffrey Hall, Kim Ho, Beng Oh and Mark Williams

La Mama Theatre is on traditional land of the people of the Kulin Nation. We give our respect to the Elders of these traditional lands, and to all First Nations people, past and present, and future. We acknowledge all events take place on stolen lands and that sovereignty was never ceded.

La Mama is financially assisted by Creative Victoria (Creative Enterprises Program), and the City of Melbourne (Arts and Creative Partnership Program).

We are grateful to all our philanthropic partners and donors, advocates, volunteers, audiences, artists and our entire community. Thank you!

La Mama Theatre & Office: 205 Faraday St, Carlton VIC 3053
La Mama Courthouse Theatre, 349 Drummond Street, Carlton VIC 3053

www.lamama.com.au   email: info@lamama.com.au
Facebook: lamama.theatre   X: LaMamaTheatre
Instagram: lamamatheatre

Office phone (03) 9347 6948
Office hours Mon–Fri, 11am–4pm.

Standing Ovation for
Australia's Home of Independent Theatre

In 2024, La Mama celebrates 57 years of nurturing new Australian Theatre, fearlessly facilitating independent theatre making.

Built in 1883 for Anthony Reuben Ford, a Carlton printer, the original building in Faraday Street had been used as a workshop, a boot and shoe factory, an electrical engineering workshop and a silk underwear factory before becoming a theatre in 1967. It was established by Betty Burstall and modelled on experimental theatre activities in New York. Jack Hibberd's play *Three Old Friends* was the first play performed in the tiny space. Since that time the crowded intimacy of La Mama has provided welcome opportunities to a host of playwrights, actors, directors, technicians, film-makers, poets and comedians, such as David Williamson, Barry Dickins, John Romeril, Tes Lyssiotis, Lloyd Jones, the Cantrills, Judith Lucy, Richard Frankland, Julia Zemiro, and Cate Blanchett... the list of both new and experienced theatre makers, and those artists who have been nurtured there, is long.

I set La Mama up, as a space for writers and directors to perform in but also it was a space where people came, as audience, to participate in the creative experiment...

—Betty Burstall, 1987

La Mama Theatre—which on various occasions has been called headquarters, the shopfront and the birthplace of Australian Theatre—was classified by the National Trust in 1999.

The two-storey brick building is of State cultural significance because it has been occupied by La Mama Theatre... The building is indelibly associated with the performance arts and is a rare manifestation of an experimental theatre in Australia...
—National Trust Classification Report.

Sadly our home in Faraday Street burned down in May 2018 and, while we were in the process of rebuilding, our home was La Mama Courthouse on Drummond Street Carlton.

Happily, like a phoenix rising from the ashes, our rebuilt La Mama Theatre was reopened in December, 2021 with the War-Rak/Banksia Festival. (For rebuild details see https://lamama.com.au/rebuild-la-mama)

During its 50 plus years, La Mama has presented approximately 2,500 shows, and we now average around 50 primary production seasons annually, as well as developments, seasonal La Mamica events (Musica, Poetica, Cabaretica, Kids' shows), regular touring through our Mobile program, plus our VCE Learning productions, play readings, and many other special events.

Performances take place again in the restored La Mama, and continue at our second performance venue, the refurbished La Mama Courthouse, 349 Drummond Street.

An ever-increasing audience is drawn to La Mama productions, not only from the Carlton and Melbourne University environs, but from far and wide across the country.

La Mama continues to be an open, accessible space, actively breaking down barriers to the Arts through diverse programs, creative initiatives, affordable ticketing, improved accessible amenities and a welcoming ethos, for performers and audience alike, that has developed over the past five decades. La Mama is home to many and open to all.

For details of all productions and events, and bookings visit: www.lamama.com.au

THE STORYTELLER® is an organic idea and was invented (designed) by Glenn Shea through his Aboriginal adolescent youth justice program via the Wathaurong Aboriginal community and has been operating for over 20 years, the cultural resource has engaged with over 200 organisation and over 50, 000 participants. The cultural resource engages with education, health and justice and provides knowledge and understanding of Aboriginal people, society and culture from an Aboriginal standpoint through active learning pathways. We deliver workshops at La Mama and each workshop delivered is specifically designed for the organisation engaging in their journey of self-discovery. We create economic development.

NGARRINDJERI

THE STORYTELLER®

WATHAURONG

Country, Language, Lore, Kinship, Ceremony

THE STORYTELLER®: Producer:
Indigenous Learning Workshops / Facilitation

Experimental Independent ATSI Theatre
An Indigenous Trilogy La Mama Theatre
MI:WI 3027 La Mama Theatre
Three Magpies Perched in a Tree
2024 VCE Theatre Studies Playlist, La Mama

PLATFORM: indigenouslearning.com.au
DVG Gollan Tangani Raukkan Coorong Ngarrindjeri

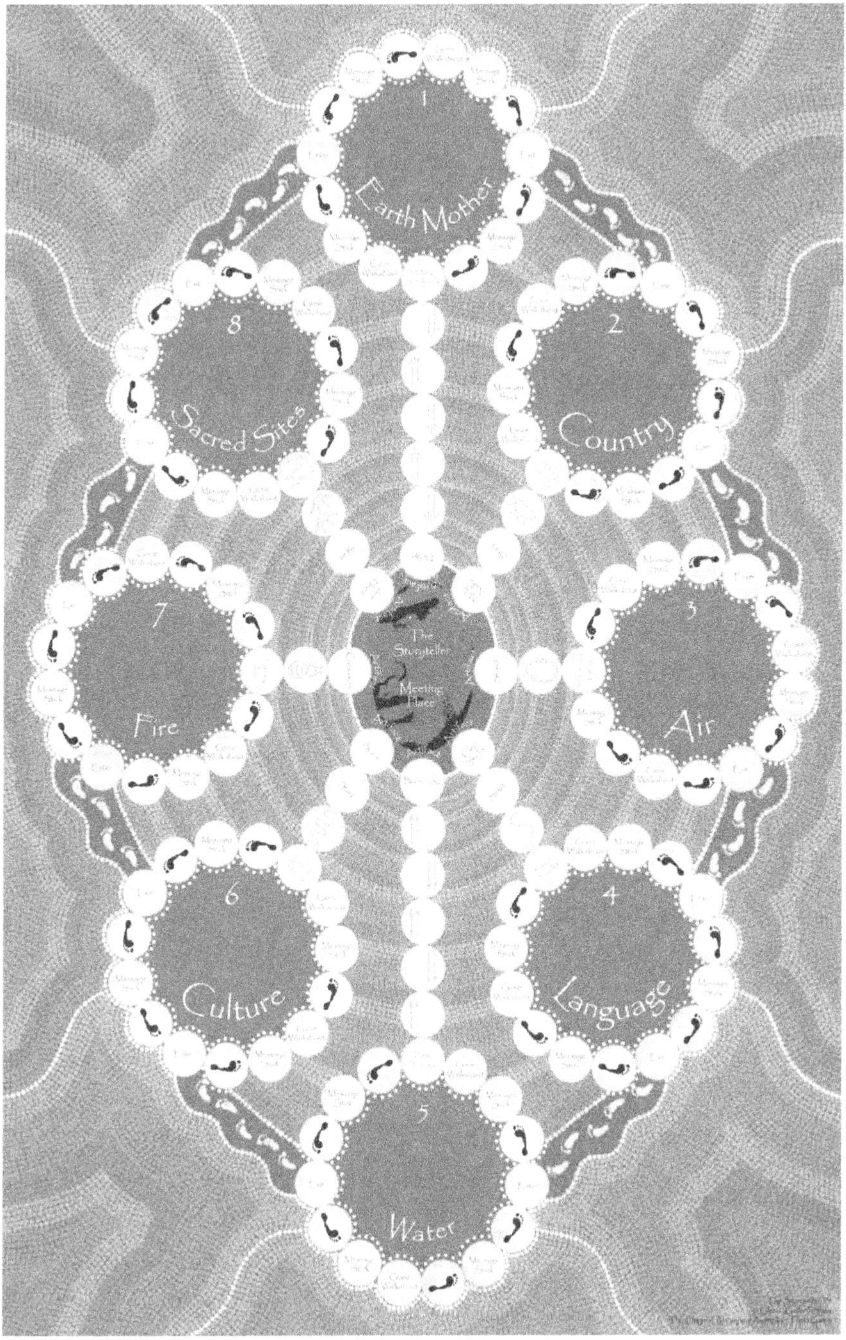
1
Earth Mother
2
Country
3
Air
4
Language
5
Water
6
Culture
7
Fire
8
Sacred Sites
The Storyteller
Meeting Place

www.ingramcontent.com/pod-product-compliance
Lightning Source LLC
Chambersburg PA
CBHW050026090426
42734CB00021B/3434